The A to Z
of
Heartfulness

For the children of the world
(and their grown-ups)

Contents

A message from Zam

Hi, my name is Zam!

Who are you?

I look like a funny robot, don't I? That's because I've connected with my heart by following The A to Z of Heartfulness.

Do you want to connect with your heart too? Then step into the book!

Oh, by the way, I need your help. Could you bring some colour to the pages and write in the special places I've left for you? I hope so.

See you after Z.

Love,
Zam

A is for Anchor

A

Ship

Drops

Down

Its

Anchor,

So as not to float away.

And I can use a calming breath,

So as not to

Sway.

Breathe...

In, two, three.

Out, two three.

In, two, three.

Out, two, three.

In, two, three.

Out, two, three.

B is for Balloon

Sometimes
I feel angry.
I feel the anger growing inside,
Inflating like a balloon ready to burst.
I feel as if I'm going to explode.
How can I release this
Pressure?

Imagine being a whale...

Take one long deep breath
And let it all go.

C is for Clouds

Thoughts
Are like clouds in the sky of my mind.
Huge, grey, gloomy clouds
Circle like hostile sharks.

Tiny, white, happy clouds
Dance like cotton puffs.

Angry, black, storm clouds
Erupt like volcanoes.

But they don't bother me...

...if...

I observe them from afar.

D is for Dream Den

There's a place that I go
When I want to be alone -
My imagination.

I build my dream den,
Beneath the branches of a willow tree,
Beside a soothing stream.

I fill it with soft cushions, books,
and chocolate.
This is all I need.

When my eyes grow heavy
I close them and listen to my breath.

All that I am thinking.
All that I am feeling,
Melts into the earth,
And we become as one.

E is for Empathy

Empathy

Means

Paying

Attention

To

How others feel,

Yourself included.

F is for Flowers

Flowers say I love you!
Flowers say I'm sorry!
Flowers say I'm sad too!
Flowers say don't worry!

Flowers speak louder than words.

Flowers...

The universal symbol of a hug.

G is for Gratitude

Gratitude means to be thankful.

What are you thankful for? Can you fill in the gaps?

I am thankful for _____.

I am thankful for _____.

I am thankful for_____.

I am thankful for_____.

Draw something that you're thankful for in the space below.

♡

H is for Happy Hearts

Happy hearts feel light,
Even when they're full.
And when we make a friend
We feel a magic
pull.

♡

Perhaps hearts are connected
By a strong invisible line,
That stretches right around the world,
And joins all hearts
To mine.

I is for Invisible

When I'm having a hard time,
I imagine that I am inside a gigantic
invisible force field.

All the vibrant colours of the rainbow
protect me.

I feel absolutely safe.

This is my ultimate superpower.

J is for Juggling

I'm juggling my emotions
Like a circus clown.
Emotions in motion!

Trust your emotions,
Your emotions are your friends.
They will guide you.

K is for Kindness

The world will be a better place,
If we help each other.
So put a smile upon your face,
Go and help another.

Now they will do a kindly deed,
For friends with extra favours.
Who with this loving kindness seed,
Will then assist their neighbours.

Deep inside your heart will grow,
You'll find much peace of mind.
And feel the gentle warming glow
That comes from being kind.

L is for Lighthouse

My heart
Shows me the way,
As a lighthouse at night.

I feel
What is wrong.

I feel
What is right.

M is for Meditation

There's no right way or wrong way to
Meditate
If you're out in the garden, then
Muditate
If you're still in your bed, then
Beditate.

There's no hocus pocus,
The breath is your focus.
Let go,
Find peace,
Don't hesitate.

N is for Nature

Nature fills me with happiness:
A thousand shades of green in springtime.
Tiny flowers that push up between the
stones.
Birdsong celebration as another day
dawns.
The soothing sound of running water and
Woosh, whoosh, whoosh of waves.
Hot sand between my toes, and the
cooling sea.
The fresh scent of cut grass, drifting in
through a window.
The sweetness of strawberries.
Bees buzzing about as I buzz about.

It's a world full of wonder,
What a wonderful world!

O is for Observations

There are lots of things I am curious about in the world. Like...

How does each seed know what flower to be?

Are you curious? What about?

Here's a space for you to record your own observations...

P is for Pebble

I make a promise to myself,
That I will be brave.
I take a little pebble,
Write the word Brave on it,
And hold it in my hand.
"I promise to be brave" I whisper.
Then I throw the pebble
As far as I can,
Out into the middle of the lake.
I watch the ripples
S p r e a d
And gently disappear
All is still.

I realise that
When I need courage,

I can go inside my heart,
Where it lies,
Waiting,
Like that little pebble.

Q is for Quiet

There's a tree at the end of my garden.
It stands tall, majestic,
Branches out wide, reaching up to the sky.
Trunk strong, roots deep.
It stands through the seasons.
Spring – the new leaves form and spread to provide shade in the summer.
In the autumn, the leaves fall in a shower of red, yellow, orange and brown.
In winter, the snow dresses its bare branches.
It sways with the gentle breeze and bends with the storm. But never breaks.

Quiet, companion, showing me that no
matter what happens,
Everything passes,
As the seasons continue to follow their
cycle.

R is for Robot

Magnetism
is a powerful, invisible, attractive force.
You can't see it,
so how do you know it's there?

Gravity is a
Powerful, invisible, attractive force
You can't see it, so how do you know it's
there?

LOVE is a
Powerful, invisible, attractive force
You can't see it, so how do you know it's
there?

Are they all perhaps the same thing?

Love is the most powerful force of all.
Use it wisely.

S is for Superhero

I want to be confident.
I want to be seen.
I don't need to be shy.

I can be a superhero!

Standing straight, I feel tall.
Hands by my sides, I feel brave.
Feet apart, I feel strong.
Chin up, I feel proud.

I don't need a cloak,
Or a cape,
Or a mask.
I can just be
ME

T is for Teamwork

Teamwork makes
Dreams work.

Bees build a honeycomb
None work alone.

Each plays his part.
For a great work of art!

U is for Universe
Poem by Trevor Murphy

Just one verse
So simple.
No more
No less
Infinite.

Then you enter.
So hard to comprehend
all this without end.

Go outwards forever,

Go inwards forever,

You are at the centre.

V is for Vision

V is i on

V is eye on

Keep your eyes on
What's around you.

There is beauty in
Everything.

W is for Whacky Walk

Feeling down? Let's turn that around...

Do the whacky walk, there's no need to
talk.
There's no need to run, come on, have some
fun.
Take a few long strides, arms out by your
sides.
There's no need for grace - pull a funny
face.

Now crouch down low, and away you go,
Jumping like a frog, off a narrow log.
Make the last jump high, up into the
sky.
Like a kangaroo, you can bounce up too.

As you start to giggle, give a little wiggle.

And a great big ROAR

Like a dinosaur.

X is for X-rays

X-ray number 999
A broken heart?
I think it's mine.

"You need some love,"
The doctor said,
"Not medicine
Or time in bed!"

♡

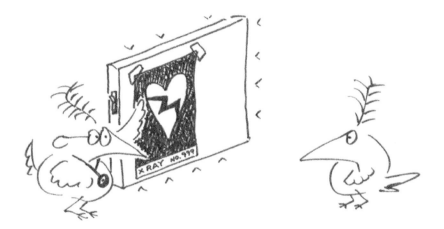

Y is for You Time

Belly rise, belly fall.
Belly big, belly small.

.

Perfect rhythm,
Steady time
I watch my breath,
And count to nine.

I feel my fingers,
Feel my toes.
Now my arms
And now my nose.

I feel so relaxed
And so at peace,
My happiness level
Does increase.

Z is for Zoom

Let's go on a journey
Let's go to the Moon
We don't need a rocket
Just Zam and a zoom.

Earth is a dot
And we're floating in space
Setting off to explore
This infinite place.

A goodbye message from Zam

Hello again,

Did you have fun discovering ways to be heartful?

Which poem did you like best?

If you enjoyed the book, please tell your friends and family about it, and leave a review on Amazon so that others can discover how to be heartful too.

Thank you!

Love
Zam

The Zend

Theme Guide for parents/educators

BREATH and MEDITATION

A is for Anchor – Using the breath for grounding

B is for Balloon – Releasing stress through breath

M is for Meditation - Meditation can be done anywhere

Y is for You Time - Awareness of the body through breath

CONNECTION WITH THOUGHTS AND EMOTIONS

C is for Clouds – Stepping back from thoughts as the observer

J is for Juggling – Handling emotions through awareness, stepping back and allowing them to be

R is for Robot – Developing curiosity about love

CONNECTION WITH SELF

D is for Den – Creating a safe place for alone time

L is for Lighthouse – Being guided by your inner self

U is for Universe – The Universe starts with you

Q is for Quiet – Time for reflection

W is for Whacky Walk – Using movement to uplift emotions

X is for X-rays – Spending time in stillness allows us to connect with our hearts

SELF - EMPOWERMENT

I is for Invisible – Strength through visualisation

P is for Pebble – Dealing with thoughts and emotions

S is for Superhero – Using posture to instil self-confidence

CONNECTION WITH OTHERS

E is for Empathy – Awareness of others and kindness to self

F is for Flowers – Flowers as a symbol of love

G is for Gratitude – What are you grateful for?

H is for Happy Hearts – The connection with others

K is for Kindness – Helping others

T is for Teamwork – Together we can create more

CONNECTION WITH THE NATURAL WORLD

N is for Nature – Appreciation for the world around

O is for Observation – Children's own observations about the world

V is for Vision – Awareness of our surroundings

Z is for Zoom – Looking at things from a new perspective

www.gotomindfulness.com

Printed in Great Britain
by Amazon